Samson the Strong Man

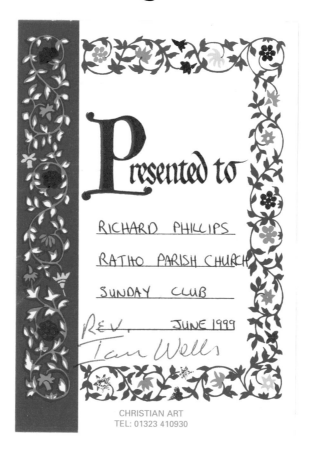

Presented to

RICHARD PHILLIPS

RATHO PARISH CHURCH

SUNDAY CLUB

REV. JUNE 1999

Ian Wells

CHRISTIAN ART
TEL: 01323 410930

Copyright © 1993 by Hunt & Thorpe
Text © Rhona Pipe
Illustrations © Annabel Spenceley
Originally published by Hunt and Thorpe 1993
Reissued in 1997
ISBN 1-85608-328-4

The CIP catalogue record for this book is available from the British Library.

Hunt & Thorpe is a name used under licence
by Paternoster Publishing, P.O. Box 300,
Kingstown Broadway, Carlisle, CA3 OQS

Printed in Malaysia

Samson the Strong Man

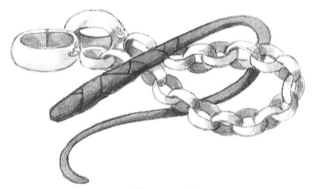

Rhona Pipe

Illustrated by
Jenny Press

paternoster
publishing

HUNT&
THORPE

'The Sea People are coming.
Quick! Hide!
They want our food and sheep.
They want to kill us!'
God's people were scared
of the Sea People
who lived by the sea.

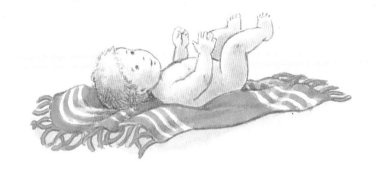

Manoah's wife was sad
because she had no children.
One day God sent an angel.
'God will give you a son.'
the angel said.
'and he will begin
to set your people free.
To show that he belongs to God
you must never cut his hair.'

Samson grew up
Super-strong.
One day he killed a lion
with his bare hands!
And one day in a temper
he killed a thousand Sea People
by himself.
He began a one man war
against them.
And they were scared of him.

The Sea People plotted to kill Samson
but he was too strong for them.
Then Samson fell in love
with Delilah.
'If you find out
what makes Samson strong,
and tell us,'
the Sea People said to Delilah,
'we will pay you well.'

'Samson, what could make you weak?'
Delilah asked.
'Tie me up with seven
new strings for a bow,'
Samson joked.
Wrong.
'Don't tease me,'
Delilah said.
'What will make you weak?'
'Tie me with brand new ropes.'
Wrong.

'Go on,' Delilah nagged.

'Tell me.'

'Weave seven strands of my hair
in your loom.'

Wrong.

'If you love me,
then tell me.

Tell me.'

Samson gave in.

'My long hair shows I trust God.'

Delilah told the Sea People.

Samson fell asleep.
His head was on Delilah's lap.
The Sea People cut off his hair.
'Samson! Samson!
The Sea People are here'
Samson woke up and said,
'I'll get free all right.'
But Samson did not know
God had left him
and he was weak.'

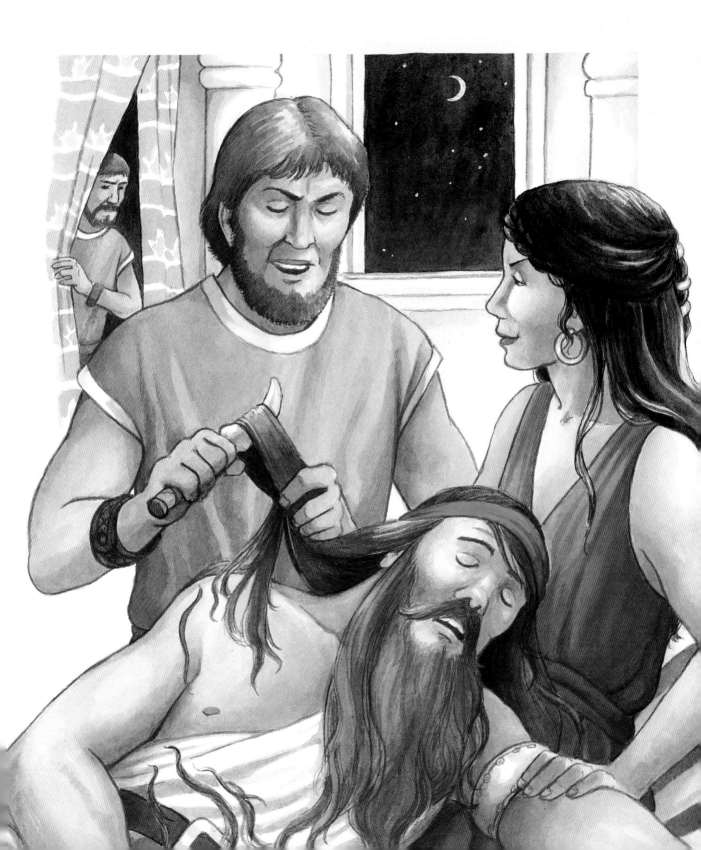

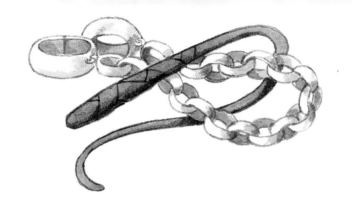

They captured Samson.
They chained him up.
They put out his eyes.
Blind Samson was made
to walk round and round
pulling a rope to grind corn.
But his hair began to grow again,
and Samson cried to God for help.

The Sea People held a party
for their god.
They got Samson from prison
and made him do tricks for them.
Samson stood between two posts
which held up the temple.
'God, make me strong again,'
Samson prayed.
'Then let me die.'
And he pushed the posts.

Down came the posts
Down came the temple.
Down came all the Sea People.
All their leaders were killed.
And Samson died happy.
He had trusted God again
and had begun to set
his people free.